Leading Others

Katie Peters

GRL Consultants,
Diane Craig and Monica Marx,
Certified Literacy Specialists

Pull Ahead Readers People Smarts

Lerner Publications ◆ Minneapolis

Note from a GRL Consultant
This Pull Ahead leveled book has been carefully designed for beginning readers. A team of guided reading literacy experts has reviewed and leveled the book to ensure readers pull ahead and experience success.

Lerner Publications Company
An imprint of Lerner Publishing Group, Inc.
241 First Avenue North
Minneapolis, MN 55401 USA

For reading levels and more information, look up this title at www.lernerbooks.com.

Main body text set in Memphis Pro 24/39
Typeface provided by Linotype.

Photo Acknowledgments
The images in this book are used with the permission of: © 3sbworld/Getty Images, p. 3; © FatCamera/Getty Images, pp. 14–15; © Jovanmandic/Getty Images, pp. 10–11, 16 (train); © kali9/Getty Images, pp. 6–7, 16 (glasses); © Pressmaster/Shutterstock Images, pp. 8–9; © tatyana_tomsickova/Getty Images, pp. 12–13; © tawan75/Shutterstock Images, pp. 4–5, 16 (trash).

Front cover: © kali9/Getty Images

Library of Congress Cataloging-in-Publication Data

Names: Peters, Katie, author.
Title: Leading others / Katie Peters.
Description: Minneapolis : Lerner Publications, [2022] | Series: Helpful habits (pull ahead readers people smarts - nonfiction) | Includes index. | Summary: "Model leadership behavior to early readers by showing how to share, how to listen, how to care, and how to give. Pairs with the fiction title Dev Makes a Card"— Provided by publisher.
Identifiers: LCCN 2020015170 (print) | LCCN 2020015171 (ebook) | ISBN 9781728403489 (library binding) | ISBN 9781728423203 (paperback) | ISBN 9781728418360 (ebook)
Subjects: LCSH: Leadership in children—Juvenile literature. | Leadership—Juvenile literature.
Classification: LCC BF723.L4 P48 2021 (print) | LCC BF723.L4 (ebook) | DDC 155.4/194—dc23

LC record available at https://lccn.loc.gov/2020015170
LC ebook record available at https://lccn.loc.gov/2020015171

Manufactured in the United States of America
1 - 48344 - 48886 - 1/22/2021

Table of Contents

Leading Others.........4

Did You See It?.........16

Index......................16

Leading Others

I can help.

I can listen.

I can share.

I can give.

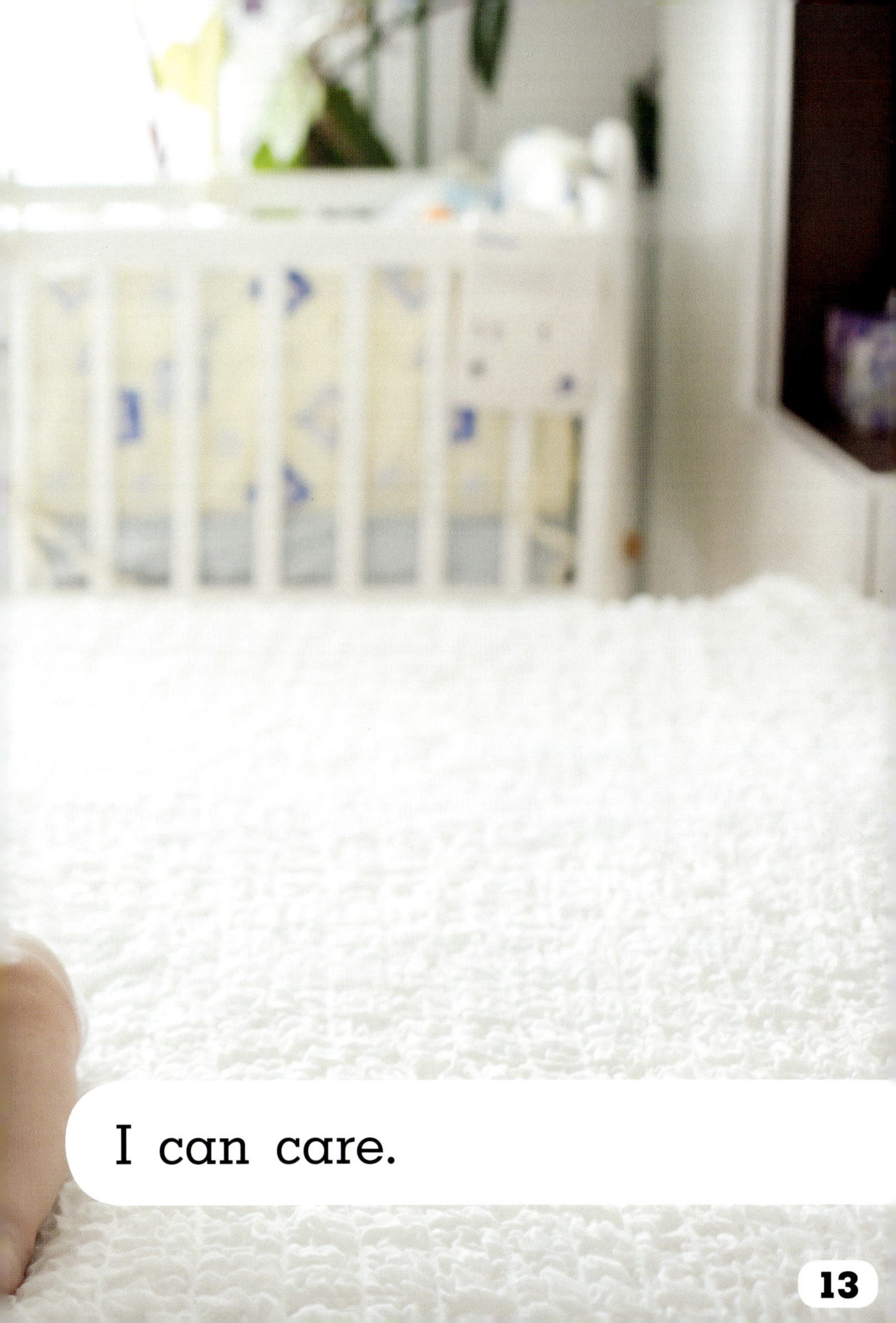

I can care.

I can lead.

Can you think of a time when you were a leader?

Did You See It?

glasses

train

trash

Index

caring, 13

giving, 11

helping, 5

leading, 15

listening, 7

sharing, 9